# THE BOOK OF
# SAUCES

# THE BOOK OF
# SAUCES

## GORDON GRIMSDALE

Photography by PER ERICSON

**HPBooks**®

ANOTHER BEST SELLING VOLUME FROM HP BOOKS®

Published by HP Books®, P.O. Box 5367, Tucson, AZ 85703       602/888–2150
ISBN: 0–89586–504–1
Library of Congress Card Number: 86–81353
1st Printing

By arrangement with Salamander Books Limited and Merehurst Press, London.

NOTICE: The information contained in this book is true and complete to the best of our knowledge. All recommendations are made without any guarantees on the part of the author or HP Books®. The author and publisher disclaim all liability in connection with the use of this information.

Publisher: Rick Bailey
Editorial Director: Elaine Woodard
Editors: Dru Ann Deger, Susan Tomnay, Beverly LeBlanc, Chris Fayers
Designers: Susan Kinealy, Roger Daniels, Richard Slater, Stuart Willard
Food stylist: June Budgen assisted by Leanne Bennett
Photographer: Per Ericson
Typeset by Lineage
Color separation by Fotographics Ltd, London–Hong Kong
Printed by New Interlitho S.p.A., Milan

# CONTENTS

# INTRODUCTION

The word 'sauce' comes to us by a roundabout route from the feminine form of the Latin word 'salsa', meaning 'salted'. Perhaps the use of the feminine gender shows that in those far off Roman times a woman's place was in the kitchen. However, the day has long gone when sauces were used simply to flavor the main ingredient, as has the myth women should do all the work in kitchens.

Larousse defines sauce as "liquid seasoning for food". Webster, however, does more for the taste buds, listing sauce as "a condiment or composition of condiments and appetizing ingredients eaten with food as a relish", or less appealing, "a fluid, semifluid or sometimes semisolid accompaniment to solid food". The great August Escoffier, "King of Chiefs and the Chef of Kings", said sauces were the secret of the supremacy of French cuisine over all others.

Definitions, however, give no hint of the enormous importance of sauces in history. Sauce creation has produced vast gastronomic and culinary effects in making plain food more palatable, or, in earlier years, unpalatable food edible. A sentence describing the nature and function of sauces could never encompass the unlimited range of textures, flavors and aromas with which sauces can assault the senses and transform simple food into gourmet fare.

This book is an attempt to simplify sauce making and to remove some of the mystery that has shrouded even the basics. It is also aimed at improving both the taste and appearance of many different types of food, from savory to sweet and spicy to tart. Follow the recipes and methods closely, but not too slavishly. Just remember, as long as certain basic rules are observed, there is always room for your own inventiveness to change a flavor subtly to suit your own taste buds.

# BROWN STOCK

bouquet garni (6 fresh parsley sprigs, 2 fresh
   thyme sprigs and 2 bay leaves)
3 or 4 lb. beef or veal shin, shank or neck bones,
   or a combination
3 quarts water
2 carrots, coarsely chopped
2 onions, halved crosswise
4 whole cloves
1 small turnip, diced, if desired
2 celery stalks with leaves, coarsely sliced
1 garlic clove
1 scant teaspoon salt
10 black peppercorns

To make bouquet garni, tie together herb
sprigs with a piece of string or place in a
cheesecloth bag; if string is used the
bouquet garni can be tied to the kettle
handles for easy removal. Place bones
and meat in roasting pan. Bake at 400F
(200C), turning once, until brown.

Place the bones and any pieces of meat
left in roasting pan in a 4-quart kettle;
add water. Stick cloves into onion halves
and add to kettle. Add all remaining
ingredients, except salt and peppercorns.
Bring to a boil over medium heat; add salt
and peppercorns. Skim surface as
necessary. Reduce heat and simmer,
uncovered, 3½ to 4 hours.

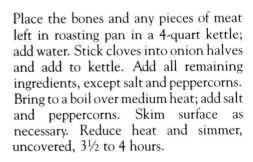

Remove bouquet garni and strain
through a fine sieve; cool. Remove any
fat that solidifies on surface. Cover and
store in refrigerator for up to 1 week.
*Makes 8 to 10 cups.*

# WHITE STOCK

1½ lb. veal or chicken bones, or a combination
   with any meat attached to them
3 quarts water
4 whole cloves
2 onions, halved crosswise
2 leeks, coarsely chopped
2 small carrots, coarsely chopped
1 celery stalk, coarsely sliced
bouquet garni (4 fresh parsley sprigs, 1 fresh
   thyme sprig, 1 bay leaf, page 8)
8 black peppercorns

Place meat and bones in a 4-quart kettle,
cover with water and let stand for 1 hour.
Bring water to a boil over high heat, skim
off foam and fat. Reduce heat and simmer
until liquid is clear.

Stick cloves into onion halves; add to
kettle. Add remaining ingredients. Bring
to a boil again; cover, reduce heat and
simmer very gently for 3 hours, skimming
as necessary.

Remove bouquet garni and strain
through a fine sieve; refrigerate until
cool. Spoon off any fat that solidifies on
surface. Cover tightly and store in the
refrigerator up to 2 weeks.

*Makes 8 to 10 cups.*

# FISH STOCK

2 lb. fish bones and trimmings
1 lb. white-fleshed fish, such as cod
1 medium onion, thinly sliced crosswise
1 leek, thinly sliced
1 carrot, thinly sliced
2 tablespoons lemon juice
bouquet garni (10 fresh parsley sprigs, 1 fresh
   thyme sprig and 1 bay leaf, page 8)
2 quarts water
12 black peppercorns
½ teaspoon salt

Place all ingredients in a 4-quart kettle over medium heat. Bring to a boil, reduce temperature and simmer gently, uncovered, for 30 minutes.

Skim off foam as required during cooking. Strain through a fine sieve; cool. Cover tightly and store in the refrigerator for up to 2 days.

*Makes 5 to 6 cups.*

VARIATION:
For a rich stock use three-quarters water and one-quarter dry white wine. Strain liquid, then return to the cleaned saucepan and boil over high heat until reduced to two-thirds.

# BASIC ROUX

A roux is made by combining equal amounts melted butter and flour with a liquid. Recipes will specify the exact quantities but the golden rule is to use equal amounts of flour and butter. Melt butter in a heavy-based saucepan over medium heat.

Add flour all at once; blend in, stirring constantly for 3 to 10 minutes (see below). Remove from heat and gradually add some of the liquid. Return to heat; beat constantly until all the liquid is absorbed and sauce is smooth and lump-free. Continue until all liquid is used, boiling and thickening sauce after each addition of liquid.

The color of the roux is determined by how long the flour is cooked; *roux blanc* is white and takes about 3 minutes; *roux blond* is a pale, sandy color and takes about 5 minutes; *roux brun* is cooked about 10 minutes until brown.

# VELOUTÉ SAUCE

3 cups White Stock, page 9
1/3 cup butter
1/3 cup all-purpose flour
White pepper and salt

Warm the stock in a heavy-based saucepan over medium heat.

Melt butter in another heavy-based saucepan. Stir in flour and cook about 3 minutes, until bubbly. Gradually add warmed stock, whisking constantly. Cook, uncovered, at a slow simmer 50 minutes to 1 hour, stirring occasionally, until reduced by one-third.

Skim any foam that rises to surface during cooking. Strain through a fine sieve. Keep hot in top of a double boiler until ready to use. Season to taste. Serve with broiled chicken breasts or lightly-cooked green vegetables.

*Makes about 2 cups.*

VARIATIONS:
**Chicken Velouté Sauce:** Replace White Stock with chicken stock.

**Fish Velouté Sauce:** Replace White Stock with Fish Stock, page 10.

**Veal Velouté Sauce:** Replace White Stock with veal stock.

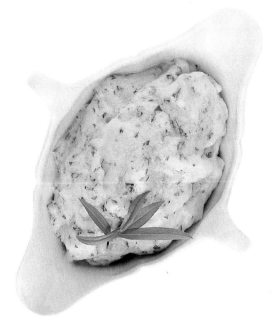

# BÉARNAISE SAUCE

1 green onion, or 1 small onion, finely chopped
2 sprigs fresh chervil
2 teaspoons finely chopped fresh tarragon, or 1
  teaspoon dried leaf tarragon
At least 4 crushed black peppercorns, or more
  according to taste
2 tablespoons white-wine vinegar
2 tablespoons dry white wine
3 egg yolks
¾ cup firm butter, cut in pieces
Salt
Red (cayenne) pepper
Finely chopped fresh tarragon or parsley, if
  desired

In a small saucepan, combine green
onion, chervil, tarragon, peppercorns,
vinegar and wine. Cook over medium
heat until liquid is reduced by half.

Place egg yolks in top half of a double
boiler over barely simmering water.
Strain onion mixture through a fine sieve
into egg yolks; whisk until blended. Do
not allow water to boil or touch bottom
of top half of boiler.

Add butter piece by piece, whisking
constantly. Make sure each piece is
melted and absorbed before adding next
piece. The sauce should be smooth like
mayonnaise. Adjust seasoning with salt
and red pepper. Stir in chopped herb, if
desired, and serve warm with roast beef,
steaks, chicken or fish.

*Makes about 2 cups.*

# MAYONNAISE

2 egg yolks
Salt and white pepper
1 teaspoon Dijon or dried mustard, if desired
1 teaspoon white-wine or tarragon vinegar, or
   lemon juice
About 1 cup olive or vegetable oil

Place egg yolks in a bowl with salt and
pepper, mustard, if desired and 1/8
teaspoon vinegar or lemon juice.

Beating constantly with a wire whisk,
add oil drop by drop at first, then in a
steady trickle until the mayonnaise is
thick. Add remaining vinegar and adjust
seasoning, if desired; stir again.

*Makes about 1 cup.*

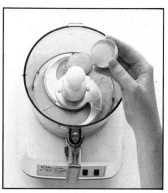

**FOOD PROCESSOR
MAYONNAISE**
Place first three ingredients and 1/8
teaspoon vinegar or lemon juice in bowl
of food processor fitted with a metal
blade. With motor running, add oil drop
by drop through hole in lid, then in a
steady    trickle    until    the    desired
consistency is achieved. Add remaining
vinegar. Do not overbeat or it will be too
thick.

*Makes about 1 cup.*

# MAYONNAISE VARIATIONS

## CURRIED MAYONNAISE

1 garlic clove, crushed
1 cup Mayonnaise, page 14
1 teaspoon curry powder, or to taste
1 teaspoon very finely chopped fresh cilantro
  (coriander) or parsley or ½ teaspoon
  coriander powder

Add garlic to Mayonnaise; sprinkle in curry powder, stirring well. Fold in cilantro or parsley. Serve with cold cooked chicken or fish. *Makes 1 cup.*

## HORSERADISH MAYONNAISE

4 tablespoons very finely grated fresh
  horseradish, or less according to taste
1 cup Mayonnaise, page 14

Stir together horseradish and Mayonnaise. Serve with hot or cold roast beef and poached or smoked fish. *Makes 1 cup.*

## MINT MAYONNAISE

½ teaspoon boiling water
3 teaspoons finely chopped fresh mint
¼ teaspoon sugar
2 tablespoons white-wine vinegar, warmed
1 cup Mayonnaise, page 14

In a small bowl, sprinkle water on mint and sugar. Crush with back of spoon to extract as much mint flavor as possible. Add vinegar; stir this mixture through mayonnaise. Serve with leftover lamb, with crisp vegetables as a dip and with salads as a dressing. *Makes 1 cup.*

## SAUCE ESPAGNOLE

¼ cup butter
¼ cup all-purpose flour
5 cups Brown Stock, page 8, warm
2 tablespoons butter
2 tablespoons bacon fat, or 1 strip bacon, finely
   diced
1 small onion, finely chopped
1 celery stalk, finely chopped
1 small carrot, thinly sliced
Bouquet garni (1 sprig fresh thyme, 1 bay leaf, 6
   sprigs fresh parsley tied together, page 8)
Salt and pepper
Strips of orange rind, to garnish

In a medium heavy-based saucepan, melt ¼ cup butter over very low heat. Add flour and cook, about 10 minutes, stirring constantly, until roux turns a rich peanut butter color: the slower the cooking the better the flavor.

Whisking constantly, gradually add stock to roux. Use a whisk to blend thoroughly. Bring to a gentle boil over medium heat, then reduce heat to low and cook, uncovered, for about 30 minutes.

Meanwhile, in a small saucepan, melt remaining butter and bacon fat. If using diced bacon, render out fat. Add vegetables and brown, stirring constantly, over medium heat. Add contents of this pan and bouquet garni to the stock. Cook, uncovered, at a slow simmer over low heat for 1½ to 2 hours. Skim any foam that rises to surface. Season to taste. Remove bouquet garni and strain through a fine sieve; cool. Spoon off any fat on surface. Garnish. *Makes about 5 cups.*

# QUICK BROWN SAUCE

¼ cup butter
2 tablespoons finely chopped onion
1 tablespoon finely chopped celery
1 tablespoon finely chopped carrot
Bouquet garni (4 sprigs fresh parsley, 1 bay leaf,
    1 sprig fresh thyme tied together, page 8)
½ teaspoon salt and pepper
¼ cup all-purpose flour
1 cup Brown Stock, page 8

In a small, heavy-based saucepan, melt butter. Add chopped vegetables and bouquet garni. Sauté gently, stirring often, 5 to 6 minutes, until vegetables begin to brown.

Add salt and pepper. Stir in flour. Cook, stirring, for 5 to 6 minutes. Warm stock in a separate saucepan, then add to vegetables. Stir constantly over a medium heat until sauce boils. When thick, simmer for about 5 minutes.

Remove bouquet garni and strain through a fine sieve. Serve hot with broiled lamb chops, pork chops or steaks.

*Makes about 1 cup.*

**Note:** If not using at once, keep in top of a double boiler over simmering water. More or less stock will produce a thinner or thicker sauce.

# BÉCHAMEL SAUCE

3 cups milk
1/3 cup butter
2 tablespoons grated onion
1/3 cup all-purpose flour
2 sprigs fresh parsley
6 black peppercorns
Pinch of freshly grated nutmeg
Salt

Warm milk in a saucepan over very low heat. Meanwhile, melt butter in another heavy-based saucepan and add onion.

Sauté onion until golden; do not allow to turn brown. Stir in flour and cook over low heat for 3 minutes or until bubbly. Gradually add milk, whisking constantly.

Cook until sauce thickens; add parsley, peppercorns, nutmeg and salt. Keep heat very low and continue cooking 20 to 25 minutes, uncovered, stirring frequently. Thin with a little extra milk, if desired. Strain through a fine sieve.

*Makes about 3 cups.*

**Note:** If made in advance, float 1 tablespoon melted butter on top. To serve, reheat in top of double boiler over simmering water; beat in butter.

# WHITE SAUCE

**2 cups milk**
**¼ cup butter**
**¼ cup all-purpose flour**
**Salt and white pepper**

Warm milk in a saucepan over low heat. In a separate heavy-based saucepan, melt butter. Add flour all at once and cook until bubbly.

Whisking constantly, gradually add milk.

Continue whisking until sauce thickens; cook 2 to 3 minutes over low heat, stirring occasionally, until the consistency is rich and creamy. Season. Serve hot with lightly-cooked vegetables or use as a base for other sauces.

*Makes about 2 cups.*

**Note:** More or less milk will produce a thinner or thicker sauce. Keep warm, if necessary, in top of double boiler over simmering water, but do not cover because the steam will thin sauce.

# TOMATO SAUCE 1

⅔ cup Brown Stock, page 8
2 lb. ripe tomatoes, quartered
8 fresh basil leaves, or 1 teaspoon dried leaf basil
Salt and pepper
Sugar, if desired

In a large saucepan, add stock to tomatoes.

Add basil and cook until tomatoes are reduced to a pulp; this may take 35 to 45 minutes, depending on ripeness. Strain through a nylon sieve. Discard skins.

Puree in a food processor or blender. Add salt and pepper and a little sugar if tomatoes are too tart. Serve hot with broiled sausages or steaks.

*Makes about 2½ cups.*

# TOMATO SAUCE 2

2 lb. ripe tomatoes
1 ½ tablespoons olive oil
½ cup finely chopped onions
1 celery stalk, finely chopped
2 tablespoons tomato paste
1 bay leaf
6 fresh basil leaves, or 1 teaspoon dried leaf basil
1 teaspoon sugar
1 teaspoon salt
Pepper

Dip tomatoes in boiling water to split the skin, then spear with a fork and peel. Quarter tomatoes and set aside.

In a medium heavy-based saucepan, heat oil over a low heat. Sauté onions and celery until onions are golden. Add tomatoes and any juice, tomato paste, bay leaf, basil, sugar and salt and pepper.

Bring to a boil. Reduce heat and simmer gently, uncovered, for 45 minutes, stirring occasionally. Remove bay leaf and discard. Serve hot with freshly-cooked pasta.

*Makes about 2 ½ cups.*

# HOLLANDAISE SAUCE

3 egg yolks, at room temperature
1 tablespoon water
2 teaspoons lemon juice
¾ cup butter, diced, at room temperature
Salt and white pepper
Paprika or red (cayenne) pepper, if desired

In top of a double boiler over low heat, whisk egg yolks, water and lemon juice until fluffy. Check water in bottom of double boiler so it doesn't touch bottom of top half or boil.

Add butter, piece by piece, making sure each piece is incorporated before adding the next; continue until all butter has been used.

Season with salt and pepper, sprinkling with paprika or red pepper, if desired. Pour into warm serving dish and serve at once with steamed asparagus, lightly-cooked fresh vegetables or poached seafood, such as salmon.

*Makes about 1 cup.*

**Note:** If sauce starts to separate, add 1 tablespoon boiling water, beating constantly. It is also possible to beat another egg yolk in a bowl and beat the separated mixture into the egg yolk; return to double boiler.

# SAUCE ROBERT

2 tablespoons butter
2 medium onions, finely chopped
2 tablespoons all-purpose flour
½ cup dry white wine
1 cup Brown Stock, page 8, or 1½ cups canned
   consommé reduced by boiling to 1 cup
1 small dill pickle
½ teaspoon red-wine vinegar
1 teaspoon Dijon mustard

In a medium heavy-based saucepan, melt butter. Add onions; sauté until soft and golden-brown. Remove onions with slotted spoon and set aside. Add flour and stir to make a roux, cooking 3 to 4 minutes, until bubbly.

Return onions to the pan. Add wine and stock. Bring just to a boil over medium heat, stirring constantly. Reduce heat and simmer for 20 minutes, uncovered.

Slice pickle, then finely chop. Add vinegar, mustard and pickle to sauce and cook 1 minute. Serve hot with broiled pork chops or roast duck.

*Makes about 1 cup.*

# MORNAY SAUCE

3 egg yolks, lightly beaten
¼ cup whipping cream
2 cups Béchamel Sauce, page 18, kept warm
1 oz. Parmesan cheese, freshly-grated

In a heavy-based saucepan, mix together beaten egg yolks and whipping cream. Add Béchamel Sauce over low heat, stirring constantly, until just boiling.

Remove from heat and mix in grated cheese; stir to melt. Serve hot with freshly steamed vegetables or cooked chicken or fish.

*Makes about 2 cups.*

**RICH MORNAY SAUCE**

2 cups Béchamel Sauce, page 18, kept warm
6 tablespoons butter
2½ oz. Parmesan or Swiss cheese, freshly grated

In a heavy-based saucepan, place Béchamel Sauce and keep warm over low heat. Just before serving, stir in butter and cheese; continue stirring until melted.

*Makes about 2 cups.*

# SAUCE VINAIGRETTE

¼ cup red or white-wine vinegar
¼ teaspoon salt
¼ teaspoon freshly ground pepper
½ teaspoon prepared or Dijon mustard, if
   desired
½ cup olive oil or vegetable oil

Use a whisk to blend all the ingredients, except the oil, together in a bowl.

Add the oil slowly, whisking continuously. When it has all been absorbed, taste the sauce; some may find the balance of ingredients too oily, especially if the vinegar is mild.

Adjust with extra vinegar, salt or pepper to suit taste. Serve with salads or crudités.

*Makes about ¾ cup.*

**Note:** Store up to 1 month in a screw-top jar in a refrigerator; shake before using.

# APPLE SAUCE

1 lb. apples, such as Golden Delicious
3 tablespoons butter
2 tablespoons lemon juice
1 whole clove
Sugar, to taste
Pinch of ground cinnamon

Peel, core and slice the apples.

In a medium saucepan, place the sliced apples; add butter, lemon juice, clove and sugar, if needed. Cover and cook over very low heat until apples are soft. Remove the clove.

Use a fork to beat the mixture gently until it is fluffy. Add a pinch of cinnamon. Serve with roast pork, duck or goose.

*Makes about 2 cups.*

# PORT & RASPBERRY SAUCE

½ cup red currant jelly
¼ cup port wine
2 teaspoons lemon juice
12 oz. raspberries, fresh or thawed
2 teaspoons cornstarch
Pepper

Spoon measured jelly into a heavy-based saucepan. Add port and lemon juice; stir over low heat until jelly melts and ingredients are combined.

Reserve a few raspberries for garnish; press remainder through fine sieve. Add puree to red currant mixture in saucepan and heat gently.

In a small bowl mix cornstarch with a little of the warm sauce. Return to saucepan and cook, stirring until sauce thickens; add pepper. Serve hot with reserved raspberries with roast game or vegetables wrapped in filo pastry.

*Makes about 1 cup.*

**Note:** If using frozen raspberries, drain well after thawing or sauce will be thin.

# RED CURRANT SAUCE

¾ cup red currant jelly
⅓ cup orange juice
½ cup finely chopped fresh mint leaves
Strips of orange peel, to garnish

In a small heavy-based saucepan, melt jelly over low heat.

Remove from heat and stir in orange juice and mint. Garnish with strips of orange peel, if desired.

Alternatively, jelly can be placed in a microwave-safe bowl and covered with plastic wrap; microwave at high for 1½ minutes, until melted. Stir in orange juice and mint.

*Makes about 1 cup.*

# SAUCE VÉRONIQUE

1 cup fish poaching liquid, or Fish Stock, page 10
¼ cup dry white wine
1 tablespoon brandy
1 tablespoon finely chopped green onion
1 teaspoon cornstarch
2 teaspoons cold water
½ cup whipping cream
Salt and white pepper
16 seedless green grapes
2 tablespoons butter, in small pieces

Boil poaching liquid, wine, brandy and green onion together in a medium heavy-based saucepan until the liquid is reduced to about ½ cup. Strain through a sieve and return to pan.

Blend cornstarch with water; add to saucepan over medium heat. Cook until bubbly. Stir in cream; cook, stirring, until sauce reaches a boil. Add salt and pepper to taste.

Add grapes. As soon as the grapes are warmed through, add butter. Blend thoroughly but gently and serve hot with poached fish.

*Makes about 1 cup.*

# PRUNE SAUCE

**7 oz. pitted prunes**
**2 tablespoons lemon juice**
**1 tablespoon finely grated lemon peel**
**8 whole cloves**
**Pinch of ground cinnamon**
**Pinch of ground allspice**
**½ teaspoon fresh grated nutmeg**
**About 1 cup water**
**½ cup sugar**
**About ½ cup red-wine vinegar**

Mix prunes, lemon juice and peel with cloves, cinnamon, allspice and nutmeg. Transfer to a medium heavy-based saucepan.

Add water or just enough to cover and heat until simmering; cook slowly about 15 minutes or until prunes are soft. Stir occasionally. When liquid has reduced to about half, take off heat and remove the cloves.

Pass through a fine sieve or puree in a food processor. Return to saucepan. Add sugar and vinegar. Cook over low heat and stir until smooth and warmed through.
Serve with roast pork.

*Makes about 2 cups.*

# BIGARADE SAUCE

1 ½ tablespoons all-purpose flour
1 ½ cups hot water
Peel of 2 oranges
1 tablespoon Curaçao, if desired
Juice of 1 orange
2 teaspoons lemon juice
Salt and pepper

This sauce is traditionally served with roast duck. When duck has been roasted, remove it from roasting pan and keep warm. Pour off any fat remaining in the pan, leaving dark meat juices.

Sprinkle on flour and stir to combine it with juices. Keep stirring over medium heat until flour is browned; add the water and bring to a boil, stirring constantly. Reduce heat and simmer 5 minutes, stirring occasionally.

Meanwhile cut orange peel into thin matchstick strips and boil them gently for a few minutes in a little water to remove the bitterness. Drain; add strips of zest to the roasting pan. Cook 5 minutes over gentle heat until the zest is soft; add the Curaçao, if desired. Stir in orange and lemon juices and adjust the seasoning with salt and pepper. Serve hot with duck.

*Makes about 2 cups.*

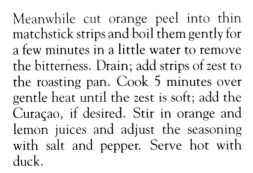

# RAISIN SAUCE

1/4 cup all-purpose flour
1 1/2 tablespoons light brown sugar
1 1/2 tablespoons dry mustard
Salt and white pepper
1 1/2 cups water
2 tablespoons white-wine vinegar
1 tablespoon lemon juice
1/3 cup seedless raisins
2 tablespoons butter

Place the first four ingredients in a heavy-based saucepan; stir to blend.

Bring water to a boil in separate saucepan and whisk into dry ingredients in saucepan, a little at a time, stirring constantly, to produce a smooth sauce. Add vinegar and lemon juice and bring to a simmer over medium heat. Cook for 7 to 8 minutes.

Add raisins. Reduce heat to low, cook 3 more minutes, or until raisins are soft and plump. Just before serving, stir in the butter until melted. Serve hot with boiled ham.

*Makes about 1 3/4 cups.*

# — ORANGE & GRAPEFRUIT SAUCE —

2 tablespoons unsalted butter
½ lb. fish bones and trimmings
2 green onions, coarsely chopped
1 small celery stalk, chopped
1 cup dry white wine
1 large orange, peeled
1 large grapefruit, peeled
1¼ cups whipping cream
Salt and pepper

In a heavy-based saucepan over medium heat, melt butter; add fish bones, trimmings, green onions and celery. Sauté over medium heat for a few minutes, stirring occasionally, until onion is golden and the celery is becoming soft.

Add wine. Simmer for 15 to 20 minutes. If liquid reduces too much, add a little water. Strain stock into a bowl. Discard bones and vegetables.

Segment orange and grapefruit. Return stock to saucepan and add orange and grapefruit segments; heat through over medium heat. Reduce heat, add cream and salt and pepper. Serve hot with broiled or poached fish.

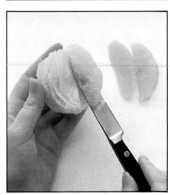

*Makes about 2 cups.*

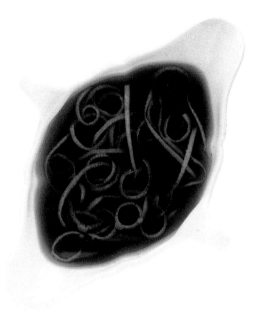

# CUMBERLAND SAUCE

1 orange
1 lemon
1/2 cup port wine
3/4 cup redcurrant jelly
1 tablespoon red-wine vinegar
Pinch of red (cayenne) pepper
Salt
1/2 teaspoon prepared mustard, if desired
6 candied cherries, finely chopped

Peel orange and lemon carefully so that no white pith is removed. Cut the peel into julienne strips. Place strips in a medium saucepan; cover with water. Cook for about 5 minutes. Strain strips; set aside.

In a medium saucepan add juice from the lemon and orange and all remaining ingredients, except the cherries. Add the drained strips. The mustard, if desired, will add an extra sharpness.

Boil mixture gently for about 5 minutes over high heat. Remove from heat and cool. Add the cherries. Serve with ham or other meat and game.

*Makes about 1 1/2 cups.*

# TERIYAKI SAUCE

1 tablespoon grated onion
3 small garlic cloves, minced
1 tablespoon grated fresh gingerroot
Salt
1 cup soy sauce
1 teaspoon sesame oil
½ cup Japanese sake, or dry sherry
¼ cup light brown sugar
2 lb. chicken or fish pieces, to serve

Place all ingredients in a small saucepan and warm gently over medium heat, stirring until sugar has dissolved.

Strain through fine cheesecloth, if desired. It is excellent as is – the small flakes of onion, garlic and ginger give it body.

Use as a marinade. Skewer pieces of chicken or fish and place in a glass bowl. Brush with sauce and set aside at least 3 to 4 hours, turning occasionally. Broil or barbecue the chicken or fish, basting frequently with sauce. Warm any remaining sauce and serve with cooked chicken or fish.

*Makes about 1½ cups.*

# ITALIAN SEAFOOD SAUCE

¾ cup dry white wine
4 oz. uncooked shrimp
4 oz. baby clams, in the shell, if desired
12 small mussels, in the shell
Pepper
Hot-pepper sauce
⅓ cup olive oil
2 garlic cloves, lightly crushed
½ teaspoon dried leaf oregano
1 tablespoon chopped fresh parsley
¼ cup brandy
4 oz. cleaned squid bodies, cut in rings
1 cup Tomato Sauce 1, page 20
8 oz. firm white fish, such as cod, chopped

In a large heavy-based saucepan, heat ¼ cup wine. Add shrimp and unopened clams, if desired, and mussels. Add pepper and a few drops of hot-pepper sauce. Bring to a boil, stirring constantly.

When mussel and clam, if using, shells open, remove and reserve; discard any which do not open. Remove shrimp and reserve with the clams and mussels. Cool, then shell. Strain; reserve liquid.

In another saucepan, heat oil and garlic until golden; remove and discard. Add herbs and remaining ½ cup wine and brandy. Simmer about 3 minutes. Add squid and simmer for 4 minutes, stirring constantly; remove and reserve. Add Tomato Sauce and bring to a boil; add reserved cooking liquid and white fish. Reduce heat; simmer 10 minutes until fish cubes are almost cooked through. Return shellfish and squid. Reduce heat and cook 1 to 2 minutes. *Makes 2 cups.*

# BLACK BEAN SAUCE

1 tablespoon fermented black beans
2 small garlic cloves, pressed
1 teaspoon sugar
2 tablespoons vegetable oil
6 tablespoons water
1 tablespoon soy sauce
1 teaspoon cornstarch
2 teaspoons water
2 large onions, sliced

Wash black beans in cold water, then strain.

Place beans on flat surface, add garlic and sprinkle on sugar. Mash with a fork to blend thoroughly. Heat 1 tablespoon oil in large skillet over medium heat and stir-fry bean mixture for 1 minute; stir in water and soy sauce. Bring to a boil, then reduce heat and simmer 2 minutes. Meanwhile, mix cornstarch with 2 teaspoons water. Stir into bean mixture; bring to a boil and cook for 1 minute. Remove from skillet and keep warm.

Heat remaining 1 tablespoon oil; add onions and cook about 5 minutes, until soft and golden. Return bean mixture and stir-fry until heated through. Serve hot with rice and stir-fried beef.

*Makes about ½ cup.*

# ITALIAN GREEN SAUCE

¼ cup fresh white bread crumbs
2 tablespoons white-wine vinegar
1 egg yolk, hard cooked
¾ cup finely chopped fresh parsley
2 anchovy fillets, drained and coarsely chopped
1 garlic clove, finely chopped
1 teaspoon finely chopped capers
About 1 cup olive oil
Salt and pepper

In a small bowl, soak bread crumbs in vinegar.

Meanwhile, place egg yolk in a medium bowl. Mash with parsley, anchovies, garlic and capers. Squeeze vinegar out of the bread crumbs and add the bread crumbs to egg mixture.

Add oil and blend until sauce is smooth and creamy. Add salt and pepper to taste. Let stand for 1 to 2 hours. Serve cold with boiled meat or steamed fish.

*Makes about 1 cup.*

# FRENCH GREEN SAUCE

½ cup fresh chervil leaves, coarsely chopped
½ cup fresh parsley, coarsely chopped
½ cup fresh tarragon leaves, coarsely chopped
½ cup chopped watercress leaves
4 spinach leaves, chopped
1 cup Mayonnaise, page 14
Few drops of onion juice
8 capers, drained and finely chopped, if desired
1 teaspoon chopped parsley

Wash herbs and spinach well. Place into a medium saucepan of boiling water and cook for 1 minute; drain.

Press with a wooden spoon in a fine sieve to extract all liquid from greens, reserving liquid. Discard cooked leaves. Set liquid aside until cool.

Carefully add liquid to Mayonnaise, taking care not to let it separate. Add 2-3 drops onion juice and the capers, if desired. Cool, then transfer to a gravy boat and garnish with chopped parsley. Serve with cooked salmon or trout.

*Makes 1 cup.*

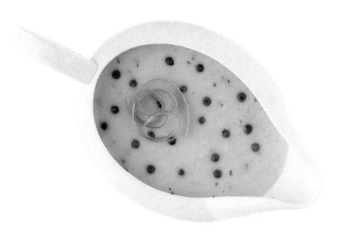

# GREEN PEPPERCORN SAUCE 1

2 tablespoons butter
1 green onion, finely chopped
2 tablespoons brandy
1 cup Brown Stock, page 8
1 tablespoon beurre manié (made from ½
    tablespoon room temperature butter, blended
    with ½ tablespoon all-purpose flour)
1 teaspoon green peppercorns, lightly crushed
2 teaspoons green peppercorns, uncrushed
3 tablespoons whipping cream
Salt and pepper

In a heavy saucepan, melt butter and green onion over medium heat until soft. Increase heat slightly, add brandy. Add stock and stir while bringing to a boil. Continue cooking until the liquid is reduced to a little less than 1 cup. Remove onions with a slotted spoon. Bring liquid back to a boil.

Add beurre manié a little at a time, using a whisk to combine well with liquid.

When sauce begins to thicken, add crushed and uncrushed peppercorns. (The best for this purpose are packed in water and sold in bottles. Remove them from the water and allow to dry before use.) Reduce heat and simmer gently for about 5 minutes. Add cream, stir well and season. Serve hot with pan-fried or broiled steaks.

*Makes about 1 cup.*

# — GREEN PEPPERCORN SAUCE 2 —

½ teaspoon green peppercorns, uncrushed
¼ cup milk
¾ cup poaching liquid, from fish or chicken, or
    White Stock, page 9
⅓ cup dry white wine
1 tablespoon Cognac
2 teaspoons Dijon mustard
¼ cup whipping cream, whipped
1 scant teaspoon green peppercorns, crushed
Salt

Place green peppercorns in a small sieve; strain, then dry on paper towels.

In a heavy-based saucepan, add milk to poaching liquid; bring to a boil. In another small, heavy-based saucepan boil wine and Cognac. When milk mixture has reduced to less than half, add wine and brandy.

Continue cooking over low heat; add mustard and cream. Stir constantly for 1 to 2 minutes. Add crushed and uncrushed peppercorns. Heat through, then serve hot with cooked fish fillets or chicken.

*Makes about 1 cup.*

# AÏOLI SAUCE

**6 medium garlic cloves**
**Salt**
**2 egg yolks**
**About ½ cup olive oil**
**2 teaspoons lemon juice or tarragon vinegar**
**Pepper**

Press the garlic cloves through a garlic press into a medium bowl. Add a pinch of salt. Add egg yolks, one at a time, and beat until combined.

Slowly drip in oil, as for mayonnaise, beating constantly. When sauce begins to thicken, stir in lemon juice or vinegar, and continue to add oil, gradually increasing to a steady trickle. Enough oil has been added when sauce becomes really thick.

Add pepper; stir well. Serve sauce with crudités or cold meats.

*Makes about 1 cup.*

# BAGNA CAUDA

6 flat canned anchovy fillets, in oil, drained
3 large garlic cloves, coarsely chopped
Salt
¼ cup olive oil
6 tablespoons butter
Pepper

Crush anchovy fillets and garlic in a mortar and pestle until they form a paste. A little salt sprinkled on the garlic will help.

Heat oil and butter in a small heavy-based saucepan and add the anchovy-garlic mixture, stirring well to combine.

Add pepper and transfer to heatproof serving dish or fondue and serve hot with fresh vegetables or Italian bread cubes for dipping into the sauce.

*Makes 1 cup.*

**Note:** If possible, try to keep hot over a flame.

# ANDALUSIAN SAUCE

1 red bell pepper
1 cup Velouté Sauce, page 12, warm or cold
1 tablespoon finely chopped fresh parsley
1 tablespoon finely chopped pimiento
2 tablespoons tomato paste
1 teaspoon lemon juice

Char pepper under broiler until black all over. Set aside until cool enough to handle. Peel off skin.

Cut pepper into lengthwise strips, then dice.

In a bowl, combine all ingredients. Serve with cold roast meats, chicken or hard-cooked eggs.

*Makes about 1 cup.*

**Note:** If you do not have time to make Velouté Sauce, substitute 1 cup Mayonnaise, page 14.

# SMETANA SAUCE

1 small onion
2 tablespoons butter
⅓ cup dry white wine
1 teaspoon all-purpose flour
1 cup dairy sour cream
2 tablespoons lemon juice
Salt and pepper

Peel and finely chop onion. In a small, heavy-based saucepan, melt butter over low heat. Sauté onion until golden.

Add wine, increase heat and bring to a boil. Continue boiling until liquid is reduced to about half its original volume.

Stir flour into sour cream. Slowly add sour cream to hot liquid, stirring constantly. Bring back to a boil briefly. Remove from heat and strain through a fine sieve; discard onion. Add lemon juice and season to taste with salt and pepper. Transfer to a gravy boat and serve hot with poultry or meat.

*Makes 1 cup.*

# PIQUANT SAUCE

1 large onion
¼ cup butter
3 tablespoons all-purpose flour
1 cup dry white wine
1 cup red or white-wine vinegar
Salt and pepper
2 dill pickles, diced
1 teaspoon finely chopped fresh tarragon
2 teaspoons finely chopped fresh parsley
1 teaspoon finely chopped fresh chervil
1 beef bouillon cube
¼ cup water

Thinly slice onion.

Turn onion to cut across slices; finely dice. In a heavy-based saucepan, melt butter; add onion and cook over medium heat until golden. Sprinkle in flour; cook, stirring, for 8 to 10 minutes until flour turns brown. Mix together wine and vinegar. Gradually add to flour mixture, stirring constantly to make a smooth, creamy brown sauce. Add salt and pepper and simmer for 15 minutes.

Add pickles and herbs. Dissolve bouillon cube in water and add to sauce; stir through. Continue simmering for 10 minutes. Serve hot with roast pork or use for reheating leftover meats.

*Makes 1½ to 2 cups.*

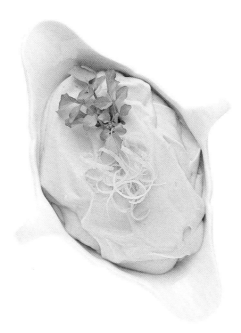

# AVOCADO SAUCE

2 avocados
⅓ cup whipping cream
⅓ cup water
½ teaspoon finely grated lemon peel
Juice of 1 lemon
Salt and pepper
4 teaspoons whipping cream

Cut advocados in half; peel and remove pits. Cut avocado flesh into pieces, then place in a food processor fitted with a metal blade. Add all ingredients, except 4 teaspoons whipping cream; puree.

Transfer to a small heavy-based saucepan over medium heat and bring to a boil. Reduce heat and simmer gently until sauce reduces to about 1 cup. Remove from heat and cool slightly. Fold in remaining whipping cream.

Transfer to a gravy boat and serve with grilled jumbo shrimp, chicken breasts or poached salmon.

*Makes about 1 cup.*

# SATAY SAUCE

¼ cup shredded unsweetened coconut
2 cups boiling water
1 large onion, quartered
2 garlic cloves
6 small dried red chilies
1 tablespoon pine nuts
1 tablespoon finely grated lemon peel
2 tablespoons peanut oil
¾ cup crunchy peanut butter
1 teaspoon sugar
Salt

In a medium bowl, pour boiling water over coconut. Stand about 30 minutes until cool. Squeeze through fine cheesecloth to make coconut milk. Set aside; discard coconut.

Place onion, garlic, chilies, pine nuts and lemon peel in a food processor or blender and puree. Heat oil in a heavy-based saucepan and add the blended mixture. Transfer to a saucepan and cook over low heat for 3 to 4 minutes, stirring.

Add coconut milk to saucepan and bring to a boil, stirring constantly. Reduce heat and add peanut butter, sugar and salt. Simmer for about 3 minutes. Serve hot over skewers of broiled marinated beef or chicken cubes. Cool, it makes a good dip for crisp vegetables.

*Makes about 2 cups.*

# – Blue Cheese Sauce & Oysters –

¼ cup butter
¼ lb. blue cheese
1 large stalk celery, very finely chopped
1½ tablespoons Worcestershire sauce
⅓ cup dairy sour cream
½ cup fresh bread crumbs
Pepper
1 hard-cooked egg, chopped
24 oysters, shucked
Lemon wedges
Fresh dill sprigs or finely chopped parsley

Melt butter in top of a double boiler over simmering water. Add cheese and celery. Cook 5 or 6 minutes, stirring frequently.

Add Worcestershire sauce, sour cream, crumbs and pepper; combine well. Cool slightly. Stir in egg.

Preheat oven to 375F (190C). Cover each oyster to top of shell with sauce. Place on baking trays and bake 8 to 10 minutes, until bubbling and lightly golden. Garnish with lemon wedges and dill sprigs. Serve hot.

*Makes 24.*

**Note:** If fresh oysters are unavailable, use canned oysters, well drained. Broil in ramekins or oyster shells.

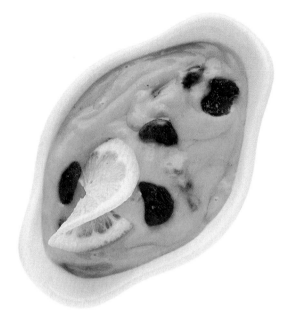

# CALIFORNIAN FISH SAUCE

¼ cup butter
¼ cup all-purpose flour
Salt
¼ cup firmly packed light brown sugar
½ cup water
Juice of 2 large lemons
⅓ cup seedless raisins
Lemon slice

In a heavy-based saucepan, melt butter; stir in flour. Stir for about 3 minutes over low heat, without letting the flour brown. Add salt and brown sugar.

Warm water and lemon juice in a separate saucepan; stir into flour and butter. Whisk to blend well; cook over medium heat for 5 to 6 minutes or until thick.

Add raisins; continue cooking over low heat until raisins are warmed through. Pour into a warmed serving bowl; garnish with a lemon slice and serve with broiled white fish.

*Makes about 1 cup.*

# CREAMY CURRY SAUCE

2 tablespoons butter
2 medium onions, finely chopped
1 garlic clove
½ teaspoon grated fresh gingerroot
1 tablespoon curry powder
2 cups White Sauce, page 19

In a medium saucepan, melt butter over low heat. Sauté onions, garlic and ginger; remove garlic clove after 1 or 2 minutes, because only a hint of its flavor is needed. Continue cooking over low heat until the onion is becoming soft and golden, but not brown.

Stir in curry powder. Cook a few minutes longer over low heat, taking care not to brown onions. Add White Sauce and mix thoroughly.

Alternatively, increase butter to ¼ cup. Add ½ cup all-purpose flour with the curry powder; stir into the onions, ginger and butter. Cook about 3 minutes until bubbly. Stir in 2 cups warm milk and bring to a boil. Serve hot, spooned over hard-cooked eggs or cooked chicken or lamb.

*Makes about 2 cups.*

# THAI GREEN CURRY PASTE

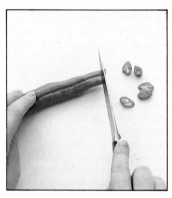

4 large, fresh green chilies, such as Anaheim
1 teaspoon whole black peppercorns
1 small onion, chopped
1 tablespoon chopped garlic
2 tablespoons chopped fresh cilantro (coriander)
2 teaspoons finely grated lemon peel
1 teaspoon salt
2 teaspoons coriander powder
1 teaspoon cumin powder
1 teaspoon ground cinnamon
2 teaspoons dried shrimp paste
1 teaspoon tumeric
1 tablespoon vegetable oil

Coarsely chop chilies; remove seeds.

Put into a food processor or blender with remaining ingredients. Blend to a paste, adding extra oil or water if necessary. *Makes about 1/4 cup*

## GREEN FISH CURRY

2½ cups coconut milk
2 tablespoons Thai Green Curry Paste, see above
1 lb. fish steaks, such as halibut, washed
2 sprigs lemon or orange leaves
1 teaspoon salt
1 tablespoon soy sauce
1 teaspoon sesame oil
1 or 2 fresh green chilies, such as Anaheim
2 tablespoons finely chopped fresh basil

Combine coconut milk and curry paste; bring to a boil, stirring constantly. Add fish, citrus leaves, salt, soy sauce and sesame oil; reduce heat and simmer about 15 minutes until fish is cooked through and flakes easily. Add chilies and basil and simmer about 2 minutes. *Serves 4.*

# CURRIED CHICKEN SAUCE

3 tablespoons vegetable oil
1 ½ lb. cubed chicken
2 onions
2 garlic cloves
2 teaspoons grated fresh gingerroot
½ teaspoon red (cayenne) pepper
½ teaspoon turmeric
1 teaspoon curry powder
1 bay leaf
2 cups small tomatoes, peeled, chopped (8 oz.)
½ teaspoon salt
2 tablespoons finely chopped fresh cilantro
    (coriander) or parsley
Hot water as needed

In a heavy-based skillet, heat oil; add chicken and brown on all sides. Remove chicken and set aside.

Sauté onions, garlic and gingerroot until the onions are golden-brown, stirring often. Add red pepper, turmeric, curry powder and bay leaf; cook for 1 to 2 minutes.

Add tomatoes and salt; mix well. Add chicken; bring to a simmer, half covered, over low heat. Simmer 30 minutes or until chicken is tender, stirring occasionally to prevent sticking. Stir in cilantro. If sauce is too thick, add a little hot water. Serve hot over boiled plain rice.

*Makes 4 servings.*

# PESTO SAUCE

1 cup fresh basil leaves, tightly packed
2 garlic cloves
Coarse or rock salt
2 tablespoons pine nuts
½ cup olive oil
2 tablespoons freshly grated Parmesan cheese
2 tablespoons freshly grated pecorino cheese, or
    2 tablespoons freshly grated Parmesan

Place basil, garlic, salt and pine nuts in a blender or food processor. Whirl until finely chopped.

With motor running, add oil in a thin stream. Scrape down sides to make sure all solids are well mixed. Continue to blend until you attain a smooth sauce.

Add cheeses and give the machine one short burst to blend ingredients well. Serve hot over freshly-cooked pasta. *Makes about 2 cups.* **Note:** Use only a high-quality olive oil and do not substitute vegetable or peanut oil. If the sauce is too thick, thin with a little of the pasta cooking water. Store any leftover sauce in a sealed container in the refrigerator for up to 1 month.

# MEXICAN-STYLE SAUCE

¾ lb. lean round beef
¼ cup vegetable oil
2 small onions, finely chopped
1 garlic clove, finely chopped
1¼ cups Tomato Sauce 2, page 21
1¼ cups water
2 large tomatoes, peeled, seeded, chopped
1 teaspoon chili powder
2 teaspoons ground cumin
½ cup grated Cheddar cheese, plus extra for serving
2 tablespoons finely chopped fresh parsley
½ teaspoon salt
½ teaspoon pepper
12 x 6-inch corn tortillas, to serve
Melted butter to serve
Shredded lettuce, to serve

Cut meat, across grain, into small pieces.

In a heavy-based saucepan heat oil; add onions and garlic and sauté until onions are light gold and soft. Add meat; cook over medium heat until well browned. Mix the Tomato Sauce and water; add with rest of ingredients. Bring just to boil; reduce heat and cook gently for 2 to 3 hours.

Brush tortillas with melted butter and warm in 350F (180C) oven for 25 minutes. To serve, equally divide sauce between tortillas. Accompany with remaining grated cheese and shredded lettuce.

*Makes about 2½ cups.*

# — CARIBBEAN CREOLE SAUCE —

½ cup vegetable oil
2 medium onions, chopped
1 medium green bell pepper, cored, seeded, finely
   chopped
2 garlic cloves
1 teaspoon finely chopped, seeded fresh red
   chilies
1 teaspoon salt
Pepper
3 tomatoes, peeled, chopped
¾ cup tomato paste
½ cup dry white wine

In a medium heavy-based saucepan, heat
oil over low heat. Add onions, green
pepper, garlic and chilies; sauté until the
peppers are soft.

Add salt, pepper and tomatoes. Cook
about 10 minutes over low heat, stirring
occasionally.

Add tomato paste and wine and simmer,
stirring occasionally. Serve the piquant
sauce hot with boiled rice or broiled
chicken.

*Makes about 2 cups.*

# — AMERICAN CREOLE SAUCE —

4 medium mushrooms
1/4 cup butter
1 medium onion
1/2 large green bell pepper, cored, seeded, finely
    chopped
1/4 red bell pepper, cored, seeded, finely chopped
4 fresh parsley sprigs, finely chopped
2 cups Sauce Espagnole, page 16
Salt and pepper
Red (cayenne) pepper, to taste

Finely slice mushrooms.

In a heavy-based saucepan, melt butter over low heat. Add mushrooms, onion, green and red peppers and parsley; cook 9 to 10 minutes until peppers are soft.

In a separate saucepan, warm Sauce Espagnole. Add to vegetables with generous amounts of salt, pepper and red pepper, according to taste. Bring just to a boil; reduce heat and simmer, covered, 45 to 50 minutes. Transfer to a gravy boat and serve hot with steaks.

*Makes about 2 cups.*

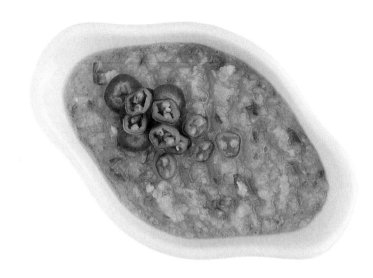

# Hot Fish Sauce

2 fresh red chilies
¼ cup olive oil
¼ cup white-wine vinegar
2 small onions, coarsely chopped
1 teaspoon lime or lemon juice
Salt and pepper

Cut chilies in half lengthwise and remove seeds; finely chop.

Place all ingredients, except the chilies, in a blender or food processor and blend until the onions are pureed into the liquid. Add chilies to onion mixture and stir through.

Transfer to a serving dish and let stand for 1 to 2 hours before serving. It will have developed its maximum zest by then.

*Makes about ½ cup.*

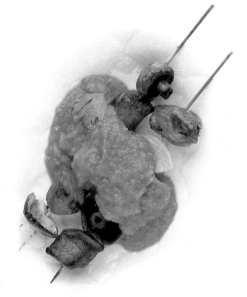

# CHILI SAUCE

10 garlic cloves
6 large onions, finely chopped
½ cup vegetable oil
7 oz. fresh red chilies, seeded and chopped
1½ cups ketchup

Peel the garlic cloves, then finely chop.

In a medium heavy-based saucepan, gently fry onions in oil until they are soft; add the garlic and cook for 2 minutes. Add chilies and simmer for about 5 minutes.

Place the mixture in a food processor; add ketchup and puree. Return mixture to saucepan and simmer 15 minutes. Cool. This keeps for several months if closely covered and refrigerated. Place what ever you immediately don't use in hot sterilized screw-top jars or bottles and store for later use. Serve as a sauce with kebabs or use as a flavoring in stews or pasta sauces.

*Makes about 3 cups.*

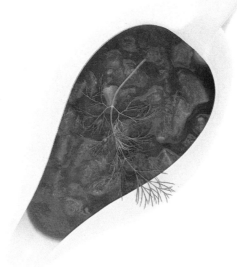

# PORTUGUESE SAUCE

1 teaspoon olive oil, or 2 teaspoons butter
1 green onion, finely chopped
1 garlic clove, crushed
4 large ripe tomatoes, peeled, seeded, chopped
Salt and pepper
2 tablespoons Sauce Espagnole, page 16, or
    Quick Brown Sauce, page 17
1 tablespoon tomato paste
Chopped fresh parsley, if desired

Heat oil in a small saucepan and sauté onion and garlic over low heat for 2 to 3 minutes, until soft but not colored.

Add tomatoes, salt and pepper, and sauté until the tomatoes are soft. Add sauce and tomato paste and bring to a simmer for 1 to 2 minutes.

Add chopped parsley, if desired. Serve hot with meat or poultry.

*Makes about 1 cup.*

# TOMATO SAUCE 3

**¾ lb. ripe tomatoes**
**2 teaspoons vegetable oil**
**1 teaspoon lemon juice**
**1 small garlic clove**
**Salt and pepper**

Boil enough water to cover the tomatoes. Pour boiling water over tomatoes and let stand for 15 seconds only. Run them under cold water, then peel. Chop and puree in a blender or food processor; pass through a fine sieve to remove seeds. Place in a bowl. Stir in oil and lemon juice.

Squeeze garlic through a garlic press into mixture.

Add salt and pepper. Stir thoroughly to combine all ingredients. Cover and refrigerate until ready to use. Serve chilled with hot or cold meat.

*Makes 1 cup.*

# SAUCE MOUSSELINE

½ cup whipping cream
1 cup Hollandaise Sauce, page 22, kept warm
2 hard-cooked eggs, shelled, cut in half, to serve

Whip cream until stiff.

In top of double boiler over simmering water fold cream into Hollandaise Sauce; gently fold until well blended. Transfer to serving dish.

Serve hot over hard-cooked eggs, or lightly-cooked fresh vegetables, such as green beans, asparagus or artichokes. The sauce also goes well with poached salmon.

*Makes about 1½ cups.*

# PARSLEY SAUCE

½ cup chopped fresh parsley
½ teaspoon lemon juice
1 whole nutmeg
1 cup Béchamel Sauce, page 18, kept hot

Place half the parsley in a small heatproof bowl; add just enough boiling water to cover. Let stand for 5 minutes, then strain, reserving the liquid.

Place the lemon juice in a small bowl; grate in nutmeg to taste. Add reserved parsley liquid; stir well.

Pour into hot Béchamel Sauce and mix through; add remaining parsley. Serve hot with seafood or vegetables, such as cauliflower or steamed carrots.

*Makes about 1 cup.*

# CHEESE SAUCE

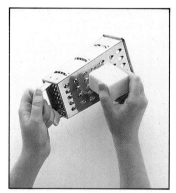

3 oz. Cheddar cheese
2 tablespoons butter
2 tablespoons all-purpose flour
½ cup milk
½ cup additional milk or vegetable cooking water
½ teaspoon prepared mustard
1 teaspoon chicken stock granules, or 1 crumbled
    bouillon cube
3 or 4 drops hot-pepper sauce
¼ cup dry sherry

Grate cheese to equal ¾ cup; set aside. In a small heavy-based saucepan, melt butter. Add flour and stir continuously over medium heat until bubbly. Combine milk with vegetable water, if using. Using a whisk, gradually pour into saucepan.

Use a wire whisk to combine into a creamy sauce. Add rest of ingredients, except the cheese, and stir gently until sauce boils and thickens.

Add cheese, stir until melted through. Transfer to a gravy boat and serve hot over lightly cooked vegetables, chicken or fish.

*Makes about 1½ cups.*

# BOLOGNESE SAUCE

¼ cup butter
1 medium onion, finely chopped
1 celery stalk, finely chopped
1 small carrot, finely chopped
¼ lb. bacon, including fat, finely chopped
½ lb. lean ground beef
Salt and pepper
Pinch of grated nutmeg
1 tablespoon finely chopped fresh oregano, or ½
    teaspoon dried leaf oregano
½ cup dry white wine
1 cup beef stock or 1 cube beef bouillon
    dissolved in 1 cup boiling water
2 tablespoons tomato paste
2 chicken livers, if desired, finely chopped
½ cup whipping cream

Melt butter in a large, heavy-based saucepan. Add onion, celery, carrot and bacon. Cook over medium heat until the onion is golden and soft.

Add beef and cook until it is no longer pink, stirring often to prevent sticking. Add salt, pepper, nutmeg and oregano. Increase heat to high and pour in wine. Bring to a boil, stirring constantly, and cook until the wine has almost evaporated. Add beef stock and tomato paste, and simmer for 35 to 40 minutes, uncovered, stirring often.

A few minutes before serving, add the chicken livers, if desired. Add cream and stir. Serve hot with freshly-cooked pasta.

*Makes about 2½ cups.*

# À LA KING SAUCE

1/4 cup butter
1/4 green bell pepper, cored, seeded, cut in short
thin strips
1/4 red bell pepper, cored, seeded, cut in short thin
strips
1/4 lb. mushrooms, thinly sliced
1/2 cup all-purpose flour
Salt
1/4 teaspoon white pepper
2 cups milk
1 egg yolk, lightly beaten
2 tablespoons dry sherry, if desired

In a large heavy-based saucepan, melt the
butter over medium heat. Add green and
red pepper strips and sauté gently for 1 to
2 minutes.

Add the mushrooms; sauté over low heat
until the peppers are soft. Add the flour,
salt and pepper, then blend. Warm milk
and pour into saucepan all at once, using
a whisk to produce a smooth sauce.

Bring sauce to a boil. Stir a little of the
hot sauce into the egg yolk. Lower the
heat to low and stir in egg yolk. Add
sherry, if desired. Serve sauce hot poured
over chicken breasts or with chunks of
hot cooked chicken for a light dish.

*Makes about 2 1/2 cups.*

# BREAD SAUCE

6 whole cloves
1 medium onion
2 cups milk
Pinch of ground mace
2 tablespoons butter
2 tablespoons cream, or use extra butter
Salt and white pepper
Pinch of red (cayenne) pepper
1 cup fresh white bread crumbs, no crusts

Stick cloves in onion. Place milk and mace in a heavy-based saucepan.

Add onion and bring to a boil. Simmer 15 minutes or more to flavor milk thoroughly. Remove onion and any loose cloves with a slotted spoon.

Add butter, cream, seasonings, and bread crumbs; beat constantly over low heat until the sauce thickens. Serve hot with roast beef or chicken.

*Makes about 2 cups.*

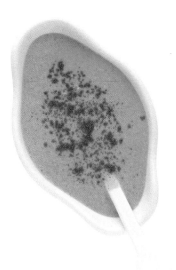

# PAPRIKA SAUCE

½ tablespoon butter
1 tablespoon finely chopped onion
1 tablespoon paprika, plus extra for sprinkling
1 cup Béchamel Sauce, page 18, or White Sauce,
    page 19
¼ cup whipping cream

In a small saucepan, melt butter over low heat. Sauté onion and paprika until onion is soft and golden.

In a separate saucepan, simmer Béchamel Sauce, stirring often, for 1 to 2 minutes. Add cooked onion and paprika.

Add cream, stirring constantly until heated through. Transfer to a serving dish, sprinkle with extra paprika, if desired, and serve hot with chicken, fish and veal.

*Makes about 1 cup.*

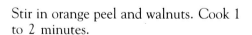

# WALNUT SAUCE

3 tablespoons butter
¼ cup all-purpose flour
¾ cup freshly-squeezed orange juice
1 tablespoon lemon juice
1 chicken bouillon cube, dissolved in ½ cup hot
    water
1 tablespoon finely shredded orange peel
½ cup chopped walnuts

In a medium saucepan, melt butter over medium heat. Sprinkle flour into the hot saucepan. Stir 3 minutes to cook the flour without browning.

In a 1-cup measuring cup, mix orange and lemon juice. Slowly add to flour mixture. Stir vigorously to avoid lumps. Add chicken stock all at once, then stir over low heat until the sauce is smooth and thickened.

Stir in orange peel and walnuts. Cook 1 to 2 minutes.

*Makes about 1½ cups.*

# CELERY SAUCE

2 to 3 celery stalks
2 cups White Stock, page 9, or 2 cups boiling
    water and 2 chicken bouillon cubes, dissolved
1/4 cup butter
1/4 cup all-purpose flour
1/2 cup whipping cream
Salt
1/2 teaspoon white pepper

Finely chop celery stalks and leaves.

In a saucepan over medium heat, add celery and stock. Cook 10 to 12 minutes or until celery is tender and soft. Drain celery and reserve cooking liquid; keep hot. In a heavy-based saucepan, melt butter, add flour and cook over low heat, stirring constantly, until bubbly. Do not let flour brown. Gradually whisk in hot celery cooking liquid.

Continue whisking until the mixture comes to a boil. Reduce heat, add celery and simmer 10 minutes. Puree in a blender or food processor; rub through fine sieve to remove strings. Return to saucepan and warm through. Add cream, salt and pepper. Serve hot with smoked mackerel fillets, cooked chicken, rabbit or lamb.

*Makes about 3 cups.*

# TARTAR SAUCE

1 tablespoon capers, drained
1 tablespoon finely chopped dill pickles
1 tablespoon finely chopped fresh parsley
1 cup Mayonnaise, page 14
1 teaspoon lemon juice
Salt and pepper

Finely chop the capers.

In a bowl, stir the capers, pickles and parsley into the Mayonnaise.

Stir in lemon juice. Adjust the flavor if necessary, with salt and pepper, or more lemon juice. Serve cold.

*Makes about 1¼ cups.*

**Note:** Store for up to week in a well-sealed container in the refrigerator; add 1 tablespoon boiling water before sealing.

# MUSHROOM SAUCE

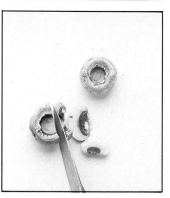

⅓ lb. mushrooms
3 tablespoons butter
2 cups Béchamel Sauce, page 18, kept warm
Salt and pepper
Paprika, if desired

Remove the stems from mushrooms and reserve for other uses. Wash the caps and dry on a paper towel.

Finely slice mushroom caps.

In a medium skillet over low heat, melt butter, sauté mushrooms until lightly browned. Add mushrooms to the just-cooked Béchamel Sauce. Season to taste with salt and pepper. Transfer to a gravy boat and sprinkle with paprika. Serve hot with chicken or fish.

*Makes 2 cups.*

# EGG SAUCE

2 eggs, hard-cooked
1 tablespoon parsley without stems, finely
  chopped
1 teaspoon lemon juice
1½ cups Béchamel Sauce, page 18, kept hot

Remove yolks from hard-cooked eggs and
rub through a coarse sieve.

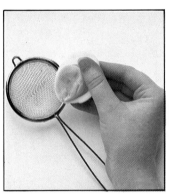

Cut whites into thin, short strips.
Combine the two. Add parsley to eggs;
set aside.

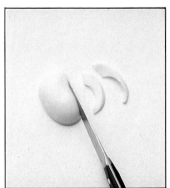

In a heavy-based saucepan over medium
heat, add lemon juice to the hot
Béchamel Sauce, stirring to prevent
separation. Add egg and parsley mixture.
Serve hot with steamed or poached fish.

*Makes about 1½ cups.*

# PEPPER SAUCE

¼ cup butter
½ large or 1 small carrot, chopped
1 medium onion, chopped
1 celery stalk, chopped
Bouquet garni (1 bay leaf, 1 fresh thyme sprig, 4
    fresh parsley sprigs, tied together, page 8)
2 teaspoons all-purpose flour
¾ cup red wine
1 tablespoon red-wine vinegar
About ¼ teaspoon freshly-ground pepper

In a small, heavy-based saucepan, melt butter. Add chopped vegetables and bouquet garni; sauté, stirring often, until vegetables are beginning to brown. Add flour all at once and stir in with a wooden spoon. Cook over low heat until flour browns, stirring constantly.

Meanwhile, warm wine and vinegar in a small saucepan. Pour all at once into flour mixture. Blend thoroughly. Bring just to a boil and simmer gently, uncovered, for 20 minutes. Add pepper to taste; cook for 1 minute.

Strain through a fine sieve and serve hot with beef or venison or other game.

*Makes about 1 cup.*

# BERÇY SAUCE

½ tablespoon butter
1 green onion, finely chopped
½ cup dry white wine
½ cup Fish Velouté Sauce, page 12
2 teaspoons finely chopped fresh parsley

In a small, heavy-based saucepan, melt butter. Sauté green onion in butter until soft.

Add wine and simmer over medium heat until the liquid is reduced by half.

Add Fish Velouté Sauce and bring to a simmer, stirring often. Mix in parsley and serve hot with fried or poached fish fillets. The sauce is also often used with fish or vegetables to be baked.

*Makes about ¾ cup.*

**Note:** To make a sauce to serve with veal, reduce Veal Velouté Sauce, page 12, by one-third and substitute for the Fish Velouté Sauce.

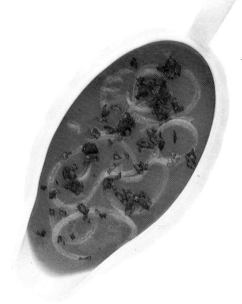

# SAUCE LYONNAISE

¼ cup butter
2 onions, finely chopped
¾ cup dry white wine
¾ cup white-wine vinegar
1 cup Sauce Espagnole, page 16
2 tablespoons butter
1 small onion, cut into thin rings
Finely chopped fresh parsley, to garnish

In a heavy-based saucepan, melt butter.
Sauté onions over low heat until they are
soft and golden-brown.

Add wine and vinegar, bring to a simmer
and cook until reduced to about 1 cup.
Add Sauce Espagnole and cook gently for
about 10 minutes, stirring occasionally.

Meanwhile, melt remaining butter in
skillet, sauté onion rings until they are
tender. Add to sauce immediately before
serving. Transfer to a gravy boat, garnish
with parsley and serve hot with pork or
lightly-cooked    vegetables    or    with
leftover meat.

*Makes about 2 cups.*

# SAUCE POULETTE

1 tablespoon butter
4 small mushrooms, finely sliced
1 teaspoon grated onion
⅓ cup dry white wine
½ cup whipping cream
¾ cup Chicken Velouté Sauce, page 12
3 egg yolks
About 2 tablespoons lemon juice
1 tablespoon finely chopped fresh parsley

Using the top half of a double boiler over medium direct heat, melt butter and sauté mushrooms until they soften. Add onion and wine and cook until wine has almost evaporated.

Reduce the heat, stir in half the cream and cook for 5 minutes or until sauce has reduced by about half. Add the Velouté Sauce and bring to a boil.

Meanwhile, in a bowl lightly beat egg yolks into remaining cream; stir in a little of the hot sauce. With water briskly simmering in bottom half of double boiler, place on top half; stir in egg and cream mixture. Cook, stirring, until very hot but not boiling. Add lemon juice and parsley. Serve hot with cooked jumbo shrimp or other shellfish.

*Makes about 1¼ cups.*

# COCKTAIL SAUCE

1 cup ketchup
1 tablespoon Worcestershire sauce
1 tablespoon grated fresh horseradish
1 teaspoon cider vinegar
1 teaspoon prepared mustard
Juice of 1 lemon
Pinch of celery salt
3 or 4 drops hot-pepper sauce
2 tablespoons whipping cream
Selection prepared seafood, such as cooked
   shrimp, to serve

In a medium bowl, thoroughly mix all the ingredients, except hot-pepper sauce and cream, using a fork to lightly beat.

Add hot-pepper sauce to taste.

Stir in cream. Cover and store in the refrigerator for up to 2 days. Serve chilled with the prepared seafood of your choice.

*Makes about 1 cup.*

# CAPER SAUCE

2 cups White Sauce, page 19, using 1 cup milk
   and 1 cup water in which ham has been boiled
   in instead of 2 cups milk
⅓ cup whipping cream
3 tablespoons bottled capers, with 2 teaspoons
   pickling liquid reserved

When White Sauce is ready, stir in
cream.

Quickly add capers and liquid. Mix
thoroughly and it is ready to serve with
lamb or ham. Do not cook any further, or
the capers and pickling liquid may curdle
the sauce.

If not serving at once, cover closely
with plastic wrap to prevent skin
forming. Reheat gently in top of double
boiler.

*Makes about 2½ cups.*

**Note:** 2 teaspoons lemon juice can be
substituted for the caper pickling liquid.

# CHÂTELAINE SAUCE

2 medium onions, finely chopped
4 large mushrooms, chopped
1 medium tomato, peeled, seeded, chopped
1 cup dry white wine
Salt and pepper
1 cup whipping cream
1 bay leaf
6 fresh parsley sprigs

Make sauce in roasting pan that has just been used for roasting chicken, duck or turkey; remove poultry and keep hot. Keep 2 or 3 tablespoons drippings in pan. In a small saucepan, cook onions, mushrooms and tomato in the white wine with salt and pepper. Simmer until the liquid is reduced to about 2 tablespoons or less.

Pour mixture into roasting pan; stir thoroughly 2 to 3 minutes, over low heat. Set aside.

In another small saucepan, combine cream, bay leaf and parsley and cook over low heat, stirring constantly, until bubbly. Add to contents of the roasting pan. Stir well and bring to a boil. Strain and serve hot with sliced poultry.

*Makes about 1 cup.*

# SAUCE SUPRÊME

1 cup chicken stock or water
½ cup mushrooms stems and pieces
1½ cups Chicken Velouté Sauce, page 12
¾ cup whipping cream

In a heavy-based saucepan, add stock and mushrooms. Bring to a boil and boil until liquid is reduced to ½ cup. Remove from heat and keep hot.

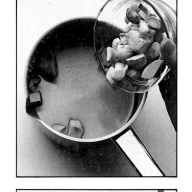

In a separate small heavy-based saucepan, heat Chicken Velouté Sauce, bring to a boil; reduce heat and simmer about 10 minutes until reduced to 1 cup. Strain mushrooms and their liquid over sauce; discard mushrooms. Stir mushroom-flavored stock into sauce.

Slowly add cream, stirring constantly. When cream is heated through, serve hot with roast chicken, poached fish or over hard-cooked eggs.

*Makes about 2 cups.*

# SAUCE CHORON

4 tablespoons dry white wine
4 tablespoons white-wine vinegar
1 green onion, finely chopped
3 egg yolks
¾ to 1 cup butter, cut into pieces
½ cup tomato paste, reduced by boiling to ¼ cup
Salt and white pepper

In a small saucepan, combine wine and vinegar; add green onion and cook over low heat until the liquid is reduced by half. Set aside to cool.

Strain and put liquid in the top of a double boiler over simmering water. Using a whisk, beat the egg yolks in until light and fluffy. Add butter, one piece at a time, stirring thoroughly after each addition. Sauce should be like a smooth mayonnaise but you may need extra butter to achieve the correct consistency.

Add the tomato paste. Season. Heat until warm, place in a serving bowl and serve with broiled meat, fish and chicken.

*Makes about 1¼ cups.*

# NEWBURG SAUCE

2 tablespoons butter
1 cup whipping cream
5 tablespoons dry sherry or Madeira
½ teaspoon salt
Pinch of red (cayenne) pepper
3 egg yolks, well beaten
Lobster coral, if available

In the top half of a double boiler over very low direct heat, melt butter and add cream. When cream is hot but not boiling, stir in 4 tablespoons sherry and season with salt and red pepper. Bring almost to a boil.

Place over simmering water in the lower half of the double boiler.

Stir in egg yolks and beat with a whisk until the sauce has thickened and is smooth. If serving this with lobster, add coral for extra flavor. Add 1 tablespoon of sherry just before serving. Serve hot at once with lobster, jumbo shrimp, scallops, roe or freshly cooked vegetables, such as cauliflower, broccoli or asparagus.

*Makes about 1½ cups.*

# CRAB SAUCE

4 oz. crabmeat, fresh or canned
1 teaspoon prepared mustard
4 tablespoons tarragon vinegar
1 small bunch fresh chives
1 cup White Sauce, page 19

Flake crabmeat, removing all cartilage; set aside.

In a bowl, combine mustard and vinegar; snip in 2 teaspoons chives, then add flaked crabmeat. Marinate for about 15 minutes.

Carefully squeeze out the vinegar and discard. In a small saucepan, warm White Sauce; add crabmeat mixture. Cook for a few minutes to gently heat the crabmeat. Serve warm with broiled or steamed fish. *Makes about 1½ cups.*

VARIATION:
By doubling the quantity of crabmeat, you can prepare a simple and delicious first course. Place the thick Crab Sauce in scallop shells and decorated with extra snipped chives and twists of lemon.

# SAUCE MATELOTE

1 garlic clove
2 tablespoons butter
½ cup Fish Stock, page 10
3 cups red or white wine
1½ tablespoons all-purpose flour
Extra butter
Red (cayenne) pepper for sprinkling

Crush the garlic by bruising it with the side of a knife.

In a heavy-based saucepan, melt 1 tablespoon of the butter and gently fry the garlic until golden. Remove garlic and add Fish Stock. Bring to a boil and reduce sauce to about half. Pour in wine and continue cooking over medium heat until the liquid has reduced to approximately 1½ cups.

Meanwhile, make a paste by combining remaining 1 tablespoon butter with flour. Add paste, a little at a time, stirring constantly. Bring to a boil. Float a little extra butter on top. Sprinkle with red pepper and serve hot with poached fish.

*Makes 1½ cups.*

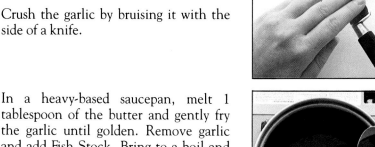
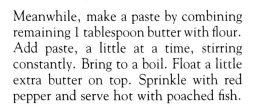

# MARINARA SAUCE

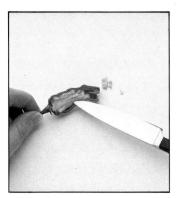

1 to 2 small fresh red chilies, such as cascabel,
  according to taste
12 large pitted, chopped, ripe olives
1 tablespoon drained capers
½ cup olive oil
1 medium onion, finely chopped
2 garlic cloves, finely chopped
2 teaspoons chopped fresh oregano or
  ½ teaspoon dried leaf oregano
1 lb. ripe tomatoes or 1 lb. can peeled tomatoes

Slice each chili and use the tip of a knife to remove seeds.

In a glass or ceramic bowl, marinate the olives, chilies and capers in 4 tablespoons oil for at least 1 hour. Meanwhile, gently sauté the onion and garlic in the remaining oil until golden. Add the oregano.

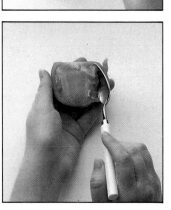

Peel fresh tomatoes; use spoon to scoop out seeds. Chop. Strain canned tomatoes. Turn all ingredients into a flameproof casserole or large skillet and cook over medium to high heat until the mixture thickens and darkens slightly. Remove chilies. Serve the sauce hot with fresh cooked pasta.

*Makes about 2 cups.*

# LEMON-MUSTARD SAUCE

⅓ cup butter
⅓ cup all-purpose flour
1½ cups chicken or beef stock, or White Stock,
    page 9
3 egg yolks
2 tablespoons lemon juice
2 teaspoons Dijon mustard
Salt
Red (cayenne) pepper, to taste

In a heavy-based medium saucepan, melt butter and add the flour all at once. Cook, stirring constantly, for 3 minutes.

Add stock all at once, using a whisk to blend smoothly. Cook over low heat, stirring often, for 5 to 6 minutes.

Gently beat in egg yolks and add lemon juice, whisking constantly. Add mustard and mix well; add salt. Cook 1 to 2 minutes longer; add red pepper, a little at a time, stirring and tasting until required degree of "heat" is achieved. Serve hot over steamed or boiled vegetables, such as asparagus, or use as an accompaniment for fish.

*Makes about 2 cups.*

# MUSTARD SAUCE

1 cup Béchamel Sauce, page 18, kept hot
¼ cup whipping cream
½ lemon
1 teaspoon prepared mustard
1 teaspoon Dijon mustard
Fresh herb sprigs, to garnish

In a heavy-based saucepan, combine Béchamel Sauce and cream. Squeeze in juice from the lemon, removing seeds.

Stir in mustards.

Serve hot, garnished with fresh herb sprigs, over broiled or poached fish or steamed green vegetables.

*Makes about 1¼ cups.*

# MINT SAUCE

1½ to 2 tablespoons superfine sugar, or to taste
2 tablespoons young, fresh mint leaves, washed and dried
1 tablespoon boiling water
½ cup red-wine vinegar or malt vinegar

To bring out mint flavor, sprinkle sugar over mint leaves.

Finely chop mint sprigs. Scrape mint and sugar into a bowl; add boiling water and stir until the sugar is dissolved.

Allow to cool a little, add vinegar, cover and refrigerate. Serve cold with lamb.

*Makes about ½ cup.*

# IVORY SAUCE

⅔ cup chopped mushrooms
White pepper
About 1 cup water
2 cups chicken or fish stock
¼ cup butter
¼ cup all-purpose flour
2 eggs
Salt and pepper
Chopped fresh tarragon, if desired

In a medium saucepan, add mushrooms, pepper and enough water to cover. Cook over a medium heat until the mushrooms are soft, strain off water and add to chicken or fish stock. Discard mushrooms. In a medium saucepan, boil this liquid over medium heat until reduced to about 2 cups.

In a heavy-based saucepan, melt butter, stir in flour and cook, stirring constantly, for 3 minutes. Add stock while still hot; continue to stir until sauce comes to a boil. Simmer for about 5 minutes, stirring often. The sauce should be quite creamy. If it thickens too much, add a little extra stock or water.

Beat eggs with 1 teaspoon hot stock. Remove sauce from heat and whisk in eggs until all frothiness has been absorbed into sauce. You should have a velvety textured, creamy sauce. Add salt and pepper to taste. Sprinkle with finely chopped fresh tarragon and serve hot with poached chicken or fish.

*Makes about 2 cups.*

# MADEIRA SAUCE

⅓ cup Madeira
1½ cups Sauce Espagnole, page 16
2 tablespoons butter

This sauce is best served with sautéed fillet mignon, chicken breasts or veal; remove the meat or poultry from the skillet and keep hot. Add all but 1 tablespoon Madeira to the skillet. Heat over low heat and stir with a wooden spoon to combine the wine with juices.

Meanwhile, in a small saucepan, simmer Sauce Espagnole over low heat until reduced to a little over 1 cup. Add to skillet, stir well while heating through.

Melt in butter. Add remaining 1 tablespoon Madeira immediately before serving. Serve hot with the cooked meat or chicken.

*Makes about 1 cup.*

**Note:** Dry sherry can be substituted for the Madeira.

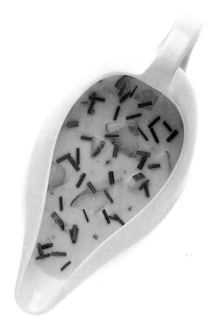

# CUCUMBER SAUCE

1 cup milk
1 onion slice
1 whole clove
½ bay leaf
1 sprig fresh parsley
¼ cup butter
¼ cup all-purpose flour
Salt and pepper
1 egg yolk, beaten
½ cucumber, quartered, sliced
½ teaspoon chopped fresh chervil
1 teaspoon snipped fresh chives

In a medium saucepan, warm milk, add onion, clove and herbs. In another saucepan, melt butter; stir in flour until well blended. Cook over low heat for 3 minutes, stirring occasionally. Season lightly with salt and pepper.

Remove onion, clove and herbs from milk; pour flavored milk all at once into flour mixture. Whisk to produce a smooth sauce. Stir continually over low heat until the sauce just begins to bubble and become thick. Remove from heat. Mix a little of the hot sauce with the egg yolk; quickly whisk in the egg yolk.

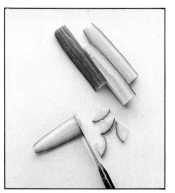

Finely chop the cucumber. Add to the sauce with the chervil and chives. Cook for 1 to 2 minutes, without allowing it to boil. Pour into a gravy boat and serve hot with seafood, such as poached salmon.

*Makes about 1½ cups.*

# Sauce Gribiche

3 eggs, hard-cooked
½ teaspoon Dijon mustard
½ teaspoon prepared mustard
Salt
About 1 cup olive oil
4 tablespoons vinegar
1 garlic clove, crushed
2 sweet pickles, finely chopped
1 teaspoon finely chopped fresh tarragon
1 teaspoon finely chopped fresh chervil
1 teaspoon finely snipped fresh chives
2 teaspoons finely chopped fresh parsley
8 capers, drained and chopped

Separate yolks from whites. Cut whites in small thin strips; set aside. Place 3 egg yolks in a bowl and mash to a paste. Add mustards and salt and mix thoroughly.

Whisk in oil, a little at a time. As mixture begins to thicken, increase oil to a slow stream, and start adding vinegar, beating constantly. Use only the amount of oil required to reach a velvety consistency, not as thick as mayonnaise.

Add garlic, pickles, herbs, capers and egg whites. Stir to mix through. Serve with cold fish, shellfish or meat.

*Makes about 1½ cups.*

# HORSERADISH SAUCE

1 piece fresh horseradish, scrubbed
2 tablespoons superfine sugar
Salt
½ teaspoon dry mustard
2 tablespoons milk
½ cup fresh white bread crumbs
¾ cup whipping cream
1 tablespoon red-wine vinegar

Cut any discolored pieces from the horseradish; cut away the outer part and finely grate 3 to 4 tablespoons.

Combine horseradish with sugar, salt and mustard in a medium bowl. In another small bowl, pour milk over bread crumbs. Mix well. Squeeze out milk, leaving crumbs moist. Add crumbs to bowl with horseradish. Stir in cream and blend.

At the last moment, stir in vinegar. Cover and refrigerate until ready to serve. The sauce will keep in a screw-top jar for up to 1 week. Serve cold with hot roast beef.

*Makes 1 cup.*

## ONION SAUCE

2 medium to large onions
2 cups milk
½ teaspoon grated nutmeg
Salt and pepper
1 bay leaf
¼ cup butter
½ cup all-purpose flour

Cut the onions into eighths.

In a heavy-based saucepan over medium heat, cook onions in milk, seasoned with nutmeg, salt, pepper and bay leaf. Cook until onions are soft. Remove bay leaf.

Meanwhile, melt butter in a medium saucepan; add flour, stirring for 3 minutes or until bubbly. Add flavored milk all at once and whisk to combine ingredients smoothly. Cook over medium heat, stirring often, until just boiling; reduce heat and simmer for 5 to 7 minutes. If desired, strain the sauce through a fine sieve; return to saucepan to heat through. Serve hot with steaks, rabbit, boiled lamb and corned beef.

*Makes about 2 cups.*

# OLIVE SAUCE

20 ripe olives, such as Queens
1/4 cup butter
1/4 cup all-purpose flour
1/2 cup Fish Stock, page 10
1/2 cup milk
1 tablespoon finely chopped fresh parsley
1/2 teaspoon finely chopped fresh oregano,
 or 1/4 teaspoon dried leaf oregano

Pit the olives, then cut olive flesh in thin strips.

Melt butter in a small saucepan and stir in flour. Cook over low heat for about 3 minutes, stirring continually, until bubbly. Warm Fish Stock with milk in a separate saucepan. Add milk-stock liquid all at once; whisk to blend into a smooth sauce. Continue whisking gently until the sauce thickens. Simmer, stirring often, for 10 minutes.

Add olives, parsley and oregano and heat through well. Transfer to a gravy boat and serve with steamed or poached seafood.

*Makes 1 cup.*

**Note:** By substituting Sauce Espagnole, page 16, for the fish stock and milk used above, you will have a rich accompaniment for lamb.

# SAUCE NANTUA

1 cup Béchamel Sauce, page 18
¼ cup light cream, scalded
2 tablespoons Lobster Butter, see below
Extra cooked lobster meat, shredded
**LOBSTER BUTTER**
1 to 2 lobster shells
1 tablespoon lobster meat
Lobster coral
2 tablespoons butter
2 tablespoons water

Begin by making the Lobster Butter; use a mortar and pestle to crush the shells, meat and coral with butter until shells are almost powdered.

Add lobster mixture to top of double boiler over simmering water with 2 tablespoons water. Cook for 20 minutes, stirring occasionally. Strain through a fine sieve into a small bowl, cover with plastic wrap and refrigerate until firm; the butter rises to the surface and solidifies. Store butter until ready to use.

To make the sauce, heat Béchamel Sauce in top of double boiler over simmering water; fold in cream. Meanwhile, melt Lobster Butter over low heat. Add to sauce with extra lobster meat. Serve hot with boiled lobster or other seafood.

*Makes about 1 cup.*

# BARBECUE SAUCE

½ cup butter
1 medium onion, very finely chopped
1 garlic clove, crushed
1 cup water
¼ cup dry red wine
1 teaspoon brown sugar
1 teaspoon salt
½ teaspoon freshly ground pepper
½ teaspoon chili powder
4 drops hot-pepper sauce
2 tablespoons Worcestershire sauce
2 tablespoons ketchup

In a medium saucepan, melt butter over low heat; add onion and garlic and cook until soft, but not brown.

Add all remaining ingredients; stir well. Bring to a boil, reduce heat and simmer for about 15 minutes.

When cooled, this may be refrigerated in a sealed jar for 2 to 3 weeks. As a sauce, it may be served cold, or reheated and served hot. Use with beef, but it is also delicious with barbecued chicken and lamb. To use as a marinade, place the meat in the liquid, cover, and refrigerate for 2 hours or more, turning the meat several times. Brush the marinade left in the dish over the meat as it cooks.

*Makes 1 to 1½ cups.*

# CHARCUTERIE SAUCE

2 tablespoons butter
1 small onion, finely chopped
1 ½ cups Sauce Espagnole, page 16
½ cup dry white wine
2 dill pickles, cut in julienne strips

In a heavy-based saucepan, melt butter, sauté onion over medium heat until soft and golden, but not brown.

Stir in Sauce Espagnole and wine; bring to a boil. Reduce heat and simmer until the sauce has been reduced by about a quarter.

Just before serving, add pickle and cook for about 1 minute. Serve hot with cooked meats, primarily pork.

*Makes about 1½ cups.*

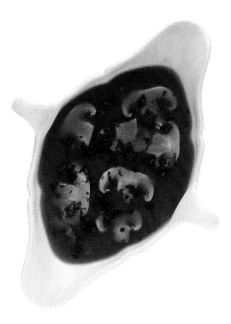

# SAUCE CHASSEUR

½ lb. mushrooms
3 tablespoons butter
½ tablespoon vegetable oil
Salt and pepper
2 teaspoons finely chopped green onion
2 tablespoons brandy, if desired
½ cup dry white wine
1 cup Sauce Espagnole, page 16
2 tablespoons Tomato Sauce 2, page 21
1 teaspoon very finely chopped fresh parsley

Wash and dry mushrooms; discard the stems and thinly slice.

In a small, heavy-based saucepan, melt butter and add oil. Sauté the mushrooms until they begin to turn light brown. Add salt, pepper, green onion and brandy, if desired. Cook over low heat for 1 to 2 minutes; add wine and simmer until liquid is reduced to little more than half.

Add Sauce Espagnole and Tomato Sauce and parsley. Heat until bubbly. Pour into a serving dish and serve hot with broiled or roast meat, chicken or rabbit.

*Makes 1½ to 2 cups.*

# SAUCE DIABLE

2 green onions
½ cup dry white wine
½ cup red-wine vinegar
¼ cup butter
¼ cup all-purpose flour
1 cup Brown Stock, page 8
Pepper
Pinch of red (cayenne) pepper
2 teaspoons finely shredded fresh herbs (parsley,
    chervil, tarragon)

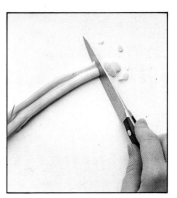

Finely chop the green onions. Place in a medium saucepan; add wine and vinegar. Simmer over medium heat until the liquid is reduced to about ¼ cup. The green onions should be very soft. Meanwhile, melt butter in a saucepan; stir in flour, stirring occasionally, for 10 minutes, until flour begins to brown. Add the Brown Stock. Whisk to blend together into a smooth sauce.

Add the stock mixture to the onions. Bring to a boil and cook for 5 minutes.

Strain green onions through a fine metal sieve; add black and red peppers. Stir in herbs. Put into a gravy boat and serve hot with broiled steaks or chicken breasts.

*Makes about 2 cups.*

**Note:** Some like a "hotter" sauce than this; add 1 tablespoon or more Worcestershire sauce when adding the wine and vinegar.

# SAUCE MEUNIÈRE

½ cup butter
1 tablespoon lemon juice, or more according to
    taste
About 2 tablespoons finely chopped fresh
    parsley
Fresh parsley sprigs
Lemon wedges

In a heavy-based saucepan over medium heat, melt the butter and allow to turn lightly brown.

Add lemon juice and parsley. Serve hot, spooned over broiled fish with parsley sprigs and lemon wedges.

*Makes ½ cup.*

## LEMON-BUTTER SAUCE

1 cup butter
3 to 4 tablespoon lemon juice
2 teaspoons Worcestershire sauce
Pepper
2 tablespoons chopped fresh parsley or snipped
    fresh chives

In a heavy-based saucepan, melt butter. Add lemon juice, Worcestershire sauce and pepper. Simmer for about 1 minute, then add herbs. Serve hot spooned over broiled fish.

*Makes 1 cup.*

# SUZETTE SAUCE

½ cup butter
½ cup sugar
1 orange
3 tablespoons orange-flavored liqueur

In a heavy-based saucepan, melt butter; stir in sugar.

Using a citrus zester, add about 2 teaspoons finely shredded orange peel; add about 1 tablespoon orange juice. Add liqueur. Bring to a boil; lower heat and cook for 1 minute.

Serve from heated pitcher over fresh fruit or ice cream. *Makes about 1½ cups.*

## CRÊPES SUZETTE
Place sauce in a large skillet. Add a precooked crêpe and warm through; fold into quarters and push to side of pan. Repeat with remaining crêpes. Add 2 to 4 tablespoons more liqueur and set alight. When flames die down, serve crêpes with remaining sauce spooned over.

# CHOCOLATE SAUCE

**4 oz. milk-chocolate candy bar**
**1¼ cups milk**
**Vanilla extract, to taste**
**1 teaspoon sugar**
**4 egg yolks, well-beaten, room temperature**

Chop or cut chocolate bar into pieces.

In a heavy-based small saucepan, heat milk, chocolate, vanilla and sugar over low heat until chocolate melts, stirring continuously. When liquid is just bubbling around the edge of the saucepan, remove pan from heat.

Spoon a small amount of the hot liquid into the yolks. Add yolks to chocolate. Return to heat and continue stirring for 2 to 3 minutes without simmering, until thickened. Serve hot with poached pears, ice cream, or steamed puddings.

*Makes about 1½ cups.*

# FRESH RASPBERRY SAUCE

**2 lb. raspberries, or other berries**
**1 tablespoon cornstarch**
**2 teaspoons orange or lemon juice**
**3 tablespoons sugar**
**Light cream for decoration**

Place berries in a food processor or blender and puree. Press through a fine sieve into a 3-cup glass measure; discard seeds.

In a bowl, mix cornstarch with a little of the juice; and set aside. Pour balance of juice into a heavy-based saucepan. Add sugar and orange or lemon juice. Heat slowly to dissolve sugar, stirring constantly. Bring just to a boil, remove from heat and stir in cornstarch mixture. Reduce heat, bring back to a simmer, stirring, and continue to cook for 1 to 2 minutes or until sauce is smooth and thickened.

Cool to room temperature. Spoon the sauce over bottom of serving plates. Carefully form a thin circle of cream around edge of sauce. Use a fine-pointed skewer to "pull" cream in opposite directions at 1-inch intervals.

*Makes about 2 cups.*

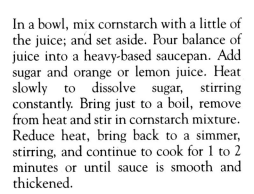

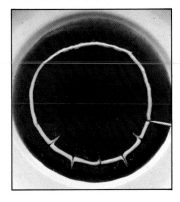

## CUSTARD SAUCE

3 tablespoons Vanilla Sugar, see below
4 egg yolks
2 cups milk, warm or scalded

Beat Vanilla Sugar and egg yolks together until light pale, smooth and creamy.

Add warm milk, stirring constantly. Transfer to top of a double boiler over barely simmering water.

Continue cooking, stirring, until sauce is thick enough to coat back of metal spoon; check frequently because the sauce can separate if overcooked. Serve hot with desserts.
*Makes about 2 cups.*

### VANILLA SUGAR
Place three 3-inch vanilla beans upright in a screw-top jar. Cover with sugar. Seal and leave for at least 1 week until the flavor has time to blend.

# — CUSTARD SAUCE VARIATIONS —

### BRANDY SAUCE
Remove Custard Sauce from heat; stir in at least 2 tablespoons brandy, whisking constantly. Serve hot with sliced fruit cake, ice cream or fruit salads. *Makes about 2 cups.*

### COFFEE-LIQUEUR SAUCE
Remove Custard Sauce from heat; stir in 2 tablespoons cold strong black coffee and 1 tablespoon coffee-flavored liqueur, whisking constantly. Serve with ice cream, sweet cookies and chilled soufflés. *Makes about 2 cups.*

### RASPBERRY SAUCE
Remove Custard Sauce from heat; stir in at least 2 tablespoons sieved raspberry puree, whisking constantly. Serve with gelatin molds, ice cream or fresh fruit salads. *Makes about 2 cups.*

# COFFEE & RUM SAUCE

½ cup hot strong black coffee
2 teaspoons sugar
2 egg yolks
⅓ cup whipping cream
1 teaspoon cornstarch
1 tablespoon milk
2 tablespoons dark rum

Place coffee in the top half of a double boiler. Stir in sugar until dissolved; cool slightly. Add egg yolks one at a time combining thoroughly after each addition. Have hot water just below simmering point in the bottom half of the double boiler, and heat coffee mixture.

Stir in cream and cook for 1 to 2 minutes.

Mix cornstarch with milk; add to saucepan and stir constantly until sauce thickens. If serving hot, add rum, stir and serve immediately. If serving cold, allow to cool, stirring occasionally to prevent skin formation. Add rum just before serving. Serve with fresh fruit.

*Makes about 1 cup.*

# Rhubarb-Berry Sauce

8 oz. rhubarb
8 oz. strawberries, hulled
½ cup sugar
Juice of 1 lemon
1 teaspoon finely grated lemon peel

Cut rhubarb into 2-inch pieces. Place in a saucepan with water to cover and cook over medium heat for 10 minutes, or until tender. Strain; discard cooking liquid.

Reserve a few strawberries for decoration. Place berries, rhubarb and remaining ingredients in food processor and puree.

Press through a fine sieve; discard seeds and any stringy pieces of rhubarb. Cover and chill until ready to serve. Place in a serving dish with reserved sliced berries and serve cold with ice cream or crêpes.

*Makes about 1 cup.*

# CARAMEL SAUCE

1 cup sugar
About ½ cup water
1 strip lemon peel

In a heavy-based saucepan over medium heat cook sugar and water without stirring until sugar is dissolved. Add lemon peel. Continue heating 4 to 5 minutes or until caramelization begins and sauce looks golden.

Have ready the saucepan of iced water and set the saucepan in it to cool quickly. This is important, as otherwise the cooking process will continue and the syrup will have a burnt flavor.

Stir to cool with wooden spoon, then remove lemon peel. Serve cold.

*Makes about 1½ cups.*

**Note:** Instead of lemon you may use orange peel, or add some brandy or Madeira just before serving. Ginger wine is nice, too.

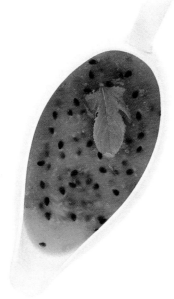

# PASSIONFRUIT COULIS

**6 passionfruit**
**2 tablespoons sugar**
**4 tablespoons water**

Cut passionfruit in half crosswise. Scoop passionfruit pulp, with seeds, into a small saucepan.

Add sugar and water.

For a thin coulis, heat until sugar has dissolved. For a thicker sauce, heat mixture to boiling point. Lower heat and allow sauce to reduce to desired consistency. Serve hot or cold with poached fruit or ice cream.

*Makes about ½ cup.*

# — MARMALADE-LIQUEUR SAUCE —

4 oz. marmalade, such as orange, lime or
   tangerine
2 teaspoons water
1 teaspoon lemon juice
2 tablespoons Grand Marnier

In a small heavy-based saucepan, combine first 3 ingredients.

Bring to a boil over medium heat.
Reduce heat and simmer over low heat
for 1 to 2 minutes, stirring occasionally.

Remove from heat. If serving hot, stir in
the liqueur and serve at once. If using
warm, cool to desired temperature, then
stir in the liqueur. Serve with crème
brûlée, fruit or a steamed pudding.

*Makes about 2 cups.*

# CHERRY COULIS

1 cup Bing cherries, fresh or pitted canned
¼ cup water, or juice from cherries
3 tablespoons orange juice
1 tablespoon lemon juice
2 tablespoons sugar

If cherries are fresh, cook in water to cover over medium heat until falling off the pits; drain. If canned, drain, reserving ¼ cup of the juice.

Place in a small saucepan with juice or water; add orange and lemon juices. Heat until warmed through.

Press through a fine sieve into a bowl. Stir in sugar while still hot. Stir until dissolved. When ready to serve, reheat over low heat. Serve with crêpes, soufflés, ice creams or sherbets.

*Makes about 1 cup.*

# LEMON SAUCE

1 tablespoon cornstarch
About 6 tablespoons freshly-squeezed lemon
    juice
¾ cup cold water
¼ cup sugar
1 lemon

In a small bowl, add cornstarch. Mix a little lemon juice with a little water and add to cornstarch. Beat to a smooth paste.

In a medium saucepan, heat remaining lemon juice and water. Add sugar, stirring constantly, until dissolved. Pour onto cornstarch paste, beating well until smooth.

Return to saucepan over low heat, stirring constantly, until thickened and clear. Using a zester, add the peel of 1 lemon. Serve hot with slices of fruit pies and tarts and ice creams.

*Makes about 1 cup.*

# SPICY HONEY SAUCE

⅔ cup maple syrup
⅓ cup honey
½ teaspoon ground allspice
1 teaspoon ground cinnamon
Pinch of caraway seeds

Mix syrup with honey in a small, heavy-based saucepan and heat over low heat while stirring.

When sauce is hot, add spices and cook over medium heat, stirring, until the sauce boils.

Serve hot from a heated pitcher with pancakes, bananas or waffles. Cool to warm, if serving with ice cream.

*Makes about 1 cup.*

**Note:** Always use the proportions ⅓ honey to ⅔ maple syrup.

# - BUTTERSCOTCH-ALMOND SAUCE -

½ cup butter
2 cups light brown sugar
½ cup whipping cream
2 teaspoons lemon juice
2 tablespoons chopped, blanched, toasted
  almonds

Melt butter in the top half of a double boiler over simmering water.

Add sugar and heat, stirring until sugar has absorbed butter. Add cream and carefully stir in lemon juice. Cook over barely simmering water for ½ to ¾ hour, stirring frequently.

Add chopped almonds. Serve hot over ice cream.

*Makes about 2 cups.*

**Note:** Chopped pecans or walnuts make pleasant variations.

# HARD SAUCE

½ cup unsalted butter
¾ cup powdered sugar
flavoring, to taste, see below

In a bowl, cream butter until soft; slowly add sugar and beat until creamy and fluffy. Add flavoring of choice.

Spread on piece of aluminum foil; chill until firm. Cut into pieces for serving.

For a festive touch, pipe into rosettes. Spoon sauce into a pastry bag fitted with a star tip; pipe 2½-inch rosettes onto a sheet of aluminum foil. Open freeze on foil, then transfer to a rigid container and layer with sheets of aluminum foil. Freeze for up to 6 months. To serve, transfer to refrigerator for ½ hour. *Makes about 1¼ cups.*

VARIATIONS:
There are endless possibilities for flavorings. For example, add a few drops vanilla, 1 or 2 tablespoons brandy or rum, or 2 tablespoons of your favorite liqueur. Add the flavoring gradually, beating constantly to avoid separation.

# — PINEAPPLE - LIQUEUR SAUCE —

½ cup unsweetened pineapple juice
¼ cup light brown sugar
¼ cup water
2 teaspoons cornstarch
¼ cup Benedictine liqueur
1 slice canned pineapple, cubed
1 tablespoon finely chopped walnuts
6 pitted dates, chopped
Pinch of allspice
½ tablespoon butter

In a heavy-based saucepan, heat juice and sugar over low heat, stirring occasionally.

Meanwhile, blend water with the cornstarch. Add to saucepan. Stir over a medium heat until sauce begins to thicken. Increase heat and bring to a boil. Reduce heat, add all remaining ingredients, except the butter, and stir for 1 to 2 minutes.

Add butter; stir to melt. Serve hot with steamed puddings, poached fruit or vanilla ice cream.

*Makes about 1½ cups.*

# APRICOT & COGNAC SAUCE

²/₃ cup dried apricots
1 cup water
1 ½ to 2 tablespoons sugar
1 teaspoon cornstarch
2 teaspoons water
¼ cup Cognac

In a small heavy-based saucepan, cook apricots with the 1 cup water and sugar for 5 to 7 minutes or until they are soft; the liquid will reduce slightly. Using a slotted spoon, remove apricots. Set aside.

Mix cornstarch with the 2 teaspoons water. Add to saucepan with apricot liquid and cook over medium heat, stirring, until the liquid thickens and clears. Transfer to a food processor or blender. Add reserved apricots. Process to a puree.

Return apricot puree to saucepan. Add Cognac and heat without boiling. Serve hot.

*Makes about 1 ¼ cups.*

**Note:** Individual preference will dictate sweetness (increase or reduce sugar), consistency (thin with boiling water if desired), and the amount of Cognac that suits your taste.

# ZABAGLIONE SAUCE

**8 egg yolks**
**½ cup sugar**
**1 cup Marsala**

In top half of a double boiler, beat egg yolks and sugar until thick and frothy.

Add Marsala and beat in. Place over simmering water in bottom half of double boiler. Make sure the water does not touch the bottom of the top half. Cook, beating constantly with an electric beater on medium speed, until mixture thickens and doubles in volume. It should have a fluffy texture. Serve hot with fresh fruits, soufflés, steamed puddings or apple or banana fritters.

*Makes about 2 cups.*

**CHILLED ZABAGLIONE:**

To serve the sauce as a dessert, remove Zabaglione from heat when it has reached the fluffy stage. Pour into a bowl and place in a large bowl of water and ice. Stir gently until cool. Transfer to serving dishes and refrigerate until required. *Serves 4.*

Charcuterie Sauce, page 99, with pork
fillets, julienne carrots and spinach
noodles

Chili Sauce, page 59, with deep-fried
shrimp and boiled rice

Green Fish Curry, page 52, with boiled
rice

Bigarade Sauce, page 31, with roast duck

Italian Green Sauce, page 38, with
steamed white-fish fillets

Velouté Sauce, page 12, with broiled
chicken breast and green beans